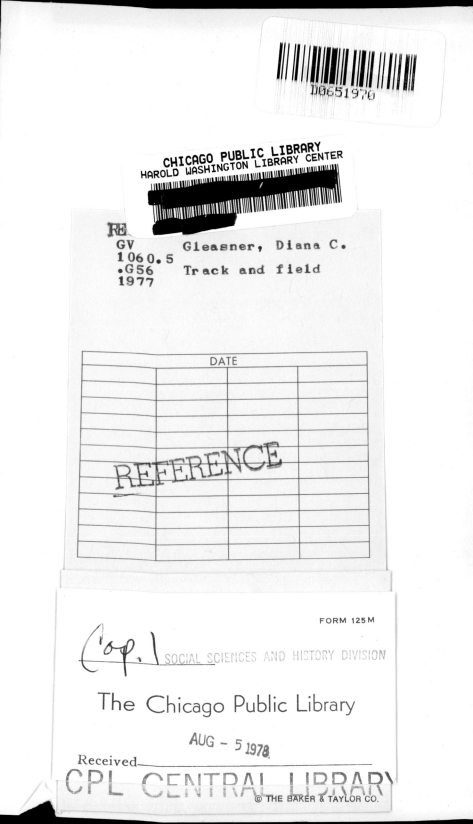

DATE		
	REFERENCE	

ABOUT THE BOOK

Women athletes have been less than welcome as competitors in track and field events, and many of those who have persisted to develop their skills, have done so in the face of prejudice and indifference on the part of athletic directors. This book focuses on the lives and careers of six women who are highly successful at distance running, sprinting, hurdling, javelin throwing, and the pentathlon. It tells of the joys and rewards their dedication has brought, and also of the obstacles each has had to overcome.

Other books in the Women in Sports Series include **Swimming, Tennis, Motorcycling,** and **Scuba Diving.**

WOMEN IN SPORTS

TRACK AND FIELD

by Diana C. Gleasner

Illustrated with photographs

Harvey House, Publishers
New York, New York

ACKNOWLEDGEMENTS FOR PHOTOGRAPHS

Arifoto: 8, 21, 24
Bob Ellis: 30
Bruce Heller USMC: 42
FMS: 8
Rick Levy: 16
Joe Matheson: 8, 31
Ralph Merlmo: 50, 53
Stan Pantovic: 55
Ingrid Schultheis: 56
Wide World Photos: 42, 45, 59, 62, 64, 67

mahalo to

The Kenmore Writers' Workshop

Library of Congress Catalog Card Number 76-55532
Manufactured in the United States of America
ISBN 0-8178-5602-1

Published in Canada by Fitzhenry & Whiteside, Ltd., Toronto

Harvey House, Publishers
20 Waterside Plaza,
New York, New York 10010

CONTENTS

FOREWORD

Running is the oldest competitive sport in the world. Prehistoric people had to outrun the wild beasts of the forests and jungles or we would not be here today. It wasn't enough to escape being eaten; man needed food. He learned to kill by hitting animals with spears or stones. From such crude beginnings developed the shot put and the javelin.

These basic survival skills were formalized by the culture of ancient Greece. The oldest recorded track event was a two hundred yard foot race in the original Olympic Games in 776 B.C. The first dozen Games featured just this one event, the classic sprint; throwing and jumping were added later. Only Greek men competed and they

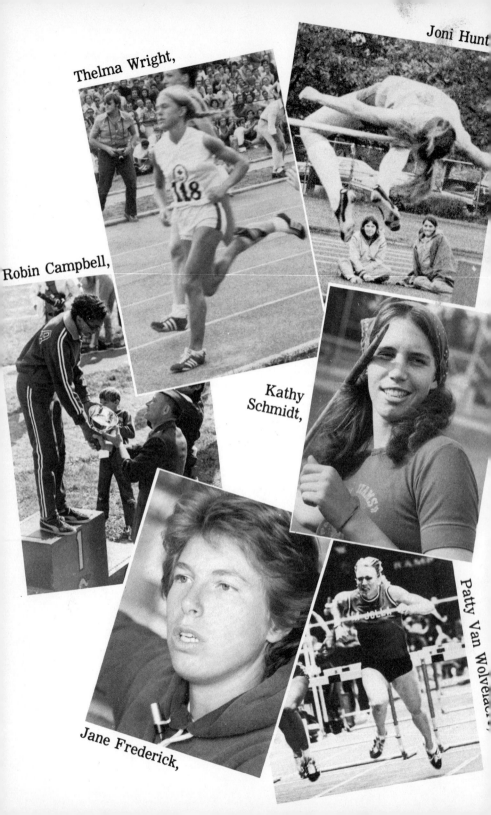

Thelma Wright,

Joni Hunt

Robin Campbell,

Kathy Schmidt,

Jane Frederick,

Patty Van Wolvelaere

ran in the nude. Women were not allowed even to watch. Any female discovered at the Olympic Games was thrown off a cliff to her death.

The Games were discontinued under Roman rule, but interest in track and field never died. The first modern Olympics in 1896 revived competitive fires by offering six track and field events in Athens. Again, it was for men only. The founder of the Games, Baron Pierre de Coubertin said, "The important thing in life is not the triumph but the struggle." But he did not believe in giving women a chance—not even a chance to struggle. He said, "Women have but one task, that of the role of crowning the winner with garlands as was the role in ancient Greece."

The Olympic Games were held every four years. Women's first involvement came in 1900 when six of them participated in a special lawn tennis competition. After that, archery, figure skating, swimming and fencing were gradually added. Track and field events were considered far too strenuous for the "weaker sex." By 1928, however, new ideas about woman's potential and her role in society had evolved and a limited track program was offered.

If people were still having doubts about fragile females, Mildred "Babe" Didrikson changed their minds. At the 1932 Olympic Games she set world records and took gold medals in the javelin throw and in the 80-meter hurdles as well as a silver medal for the high jump.

Of the many outstanding female performances in the Olympics, the greatest were by Fanny Blankers-Koen in 1948. Before the Games this Dutch mother of two had set world records in the long and the high jumps. Since she already knew she was number one in jumping, she decided to test her skills in other areas. She entered the 80-

meter hurdles, the 100 and 200-meter races and ran anchor position in the 400-meter relay. She won them all and became the fourth athlete and the only woman in Olympic history to win four gold medals.

In spite of these memorable female victories, track and field was considered a controversial activity for many years. Ellen Cornish, an outstanding American distance runner, wasn't allowed to compete on her high school team because she was a girl. In the spring of 1972 officials let her run in only one meet providing the points she earned wouldn't count for her school. At the end of the seventh lap with Ellen fighting for the lead, she was pulled from the track. The coaches had planned to do this to protect the boys from the shame of being beaten by a girl.

In 1967 Kathy Switzer, dressed in a loose-fitting sweat suit and with an entry blank marked "K. Switzer," entered the Boston Marathon. When it was discovered that she was a female her number was ripped from her back and she was shoved from the course. Yet Kathy went the distance.

A judge in a 1971 Connecticut court case denied women the right to participate on a cross country team because "...athletic competition builds character in our boys. We do not need that kind of character in our girls, the women of tomorrow."

Only a few years ago women who competed in track and field were laughed at, leered at, sworn at and told to go home and act like ladies. Even today women athletes are accepted in the United States far less readily than in the countries of Eastern and Western Europe, as witnessed by the stunning performances of the European

Women at the 1976 Montreal Olympics. Until sports are encouraged and promoted for American females as highly as they are for men, there will be prejudices to overcome.

Some of the myths of female inferiority are already crumbling. Studies show that the idea of the fragile female is fiction. Women thrive on physical activity. Doctors are now saying what female runners have known for years: running feels good.

Famed new Zealand coach Arthur Lydiard wrote in the 1960's that women could run as far as men and could train seven days a week all year even though it had been considered unwise, if not impossible, only a few years before.

Dr. Joan Ullyot said, "In long races there's less chance of women hurting themselves than men. Women have the endurance and better metabolism. After twenty miles, women utilize their fat better. By then all the carbohydrates have been burned up."

Years ago, women went to bed when they were menstruating. Today, activity during that time is considered normal and healthy. Women continue to train and compete without complaint. One study done at the Tokyo Olympics showed that women contestants won gold medals during all phases of the menstrual cycle.

Several women have won Olympic medals while pregnant. And many have come back after childbirth to compete and win. Paola Cacchi and Joyce Smith both interrupted running careers to have babies. Yet they finished first and second in the '73 International Cross-Country Championship. Judy Pollack found that at thirty-one, after three children, she could run as fast as she did when she set the world half-mile record. Miki Gorman who ran in the New York City Marathon eight months after a difficult delivery said, "After the baby, the marathon's nothing."

Girls and women in track and field learn to take problems in their stride. Achievement usually has a price tag. The price in this sport is discipline, hard work, and pain. Serious competitors learn to make choices. They give up parties and leisure time to accept the rigors of conditioning. In return they have the pleasure of living in finely-tuned bodies and the satisfaction of developing their potential to the fullest.

Track and field athletes learn to handle pain. Javelin thrower Kathy Schmidt says matter-of-factly, "I can't remember a time when my elbow didn't hurt." Runners speak of two kinds of pain, one a warning, the other a challenge. They learn to distinguish between the two and welcome the pain of challenge. Through pain comes growth and new levels of achievement.

Women who have overcome prejudices against their sex and have made the daily sacrifices that training involves have other problems to face as well. One major stumbling block is money. Olympic competitors must be amateurs. The official definition of amateur is "one who participates solely for pleasure and for the physical, mental and social benefits he derives therefrom, and to whom participation is nothing more than recreation without material gain of any kind, direct or indirect." This definition, if taken literally, would exclude all athletes from the iron curtain countries and most others, including Americans, from competing under amateur status.

Francie Larrieux, a great American distance runner, resents the Amateur Athletic Union's rules. "If they were to help me out," she says, "so I wouldn't have to worry where my next meal is coming from, that would be different. I'm supporting myself and then they come in and tell me when I can run and when I can't."

Some women have solved the perennial problem of how to support themselves by running for money rather than for glory on the professional track circuit. Runner Wyomia Tyus Simburg says she ended a five-year retirement to join the International Track Association tour because "I was deeply concerned about women's track and field in this country. This way we can be paid for our service as in any other field." Barbara Ferrell also chose to go professional. "I don't need to beg people for contributions for travel to the AAU Nationals the way the amateurs do," she says.

While there are plenty of problems, track and field offers many rewards. Women need not compete at the Olympic level to derive great satisfaction from the sport. Because of the variety of activities in track and field, there are opportunies for all girls, short, tall, fast, heavy, slow, strong and weak. And since these are individualized sports, each girl has a chance to express her own unique personality.

The physical benefits are many. The circulatory and respiratory systems are improved, weight is more easily controlled, in fact all physical, mental and emotional development makes great gains. The feeling of well being that comes from strenuous exercise is reason enough to participate. Those who learn to persevere despite many difficulties will reap the rewards of winning and the self-esteem that comes from proving equal to challenges.

Some women have overcome serious physical handicaps and gone on to successful athletic careers. Wilma Rudolf caught pneumonia and scarlet fever at the same time when she was just four years old. As a result she lost the use of one leg. She was soon hopping around on one foot and later, with the help of special shoes, learned to walk again. In high school she discovered track and decided she would do whatever she must to become a winner. In the 1960 Olympics, just sixteen years after she was unable to walk, she ran away with three gold medals.

This sort of fierce determination to succeed is the difference between winners and other competitors. Cheryl Toussaint had only been in training for two weeks when she was entered in a one-mile race. Her coach reminded her that she wasn't in condition and that her goal should be to try to finish. Cheryl wanted more than competitive experience. She wanted to win. But her lack of conditioning caught up with her about a hundred yards from the finish and she collapsed. She stood, staggered and fell again. Still ahead of the other runners she started to crawl toward the finish line on her hands and knees. Alternate staggering and crawling earned her a second place. Her coach predicted great things for Cheryl, who went on to a silver medal in the '68 Olympics and a new world record for the 600-yard run.

Opportunities for women in track and field are increasing at an impressive rate. Five years after they ripped Kathy Switzer's number from her back, the Boston Marathon officially welcomed women participants. On the horizon are running scholarships, levels of competition comparable to those offered men, equal media time, and new positions on the professional circuit.

Women in track and field are racing toward equality, a race where everyone is a winner.

ONE Thelma Wright

Thelma took her place at the starting line beside sixty-nine other competitors from eighteen countries. She felt sick to her stomach. She thought of the turtle steak she'd been served the night before, then told herself firmly that it was just her usual case of pre-race jitters. Nothing to worry about.

The sun blazed on her head. It was two o'clock, ninety-five degrees and not a cloud in the sky. A huge sweating crowd milled about waiting impatiently for the start of the International Feminine 10,000 Meter Road Race. It seemed as if all of Puerto Rico had turned out for the event. People were everywhere, even on the rooftops. Thelma wanted to show them all what a Canadian woman could do.

But ten minutes of just standing in the white glare drained Thelma. Her arms and legs were prickly and she felt too tired to move. It took great effort just to hold her eyelids open. She pushed her fatigue from her mind and said over and over to herself, All I have to do is run 6¼ miles. No problem.

15

Thelma Wright at the Springbank Road Races,
London, Ontario, September, 1974

To a cross country runner 6¼ miles is just another day's work, especially to Thelma Wright, who used to run the five miles to her high school friend's house every night just for fun. But that was in Canada, where it was cool. She struggled to keep her eyes open. Would she ever feel cool again?

The gun barked. Move, legs! Thelma silently ordered. Helplessly she watched the barefoot girls from the island of Barbados streak away from her. The three Canadian girls had planned to start out briskly but those plans seemed a lifetime away. Just keep going, she thought, wishing as always that she was taller than five feet. She could surely use longer legs today.

The first three miles were uphill. Thelma reached her stride and settled into the race. Six and one-quarter miles, no problem, she told herself and concentrated on the slope ahead. Her stomach was okay. She ran faster. As she caught up to and passed the barefoot girls she thought, "Now, just survive the heat.

Thelma's mind ran along with her legs. She had arrived in pouring rain. No one had met her group at the airport. Phones were out of order due to the storm. The crowds were terrible. Noisy fireworks made sleep impossible. It was impossible anyway in the unfinished housing development in which she'd been housed. It had no furniture, not even beds. The floors were muddy; the toilets flooded, and there was no paper. She was exhausted. She had slept fitfully on the floor.

Then there was the femininity test to be sure no men tried to compete as women. It was not the usual test using a scraping from her mouth. It was humiliating to have to disrobe and be examined. But that was not as bad as the hairy black spider on the ceiling. She could still see it.

Thelma's legs felt heavy but she was now in the lead. Her face burned. Somehow running was far less complicated than yesterday's problems.

After the femininity test, there had been a physical examination. Because she was born with a hole between the walls of her heart and her elementary school record showed a nurse's report that said she had a heart murmur, yesterday's doctors said, No, this woman can not compete.

Thelma had pleaded. There had been a thirty-mile drive to the hospital followed by an electrocardiogram. After an hour's wait while five doctors consulted, they had said she was unfit to run.

"But I've been in many international games," Thelma had protested. "I've been running for eight years. Ten miles a day."

"In that case," one of the doctors had said, "only if an ambulance follows all the way. And if you feel sick . . ."

"I'll stop. I promise." She had almost cried with relief.

She felt lighter now. She passed the half way mark, had turned, and was heading back. Four miles done—two and a quarter to go. If only the ambulance would disappear. And the motorcycle police. Sickening fumes from the vehicles seared her lungs. But the crowd took her mind off the fumes. Glasses of water were thrust out to her. Her throat was raw but she couldn't drink. The spectators wanted to help. They began to throw water at the overheated runners. Someone aimed a hose right in her face. The water went up her nose and choked her. Coughing, but running, she held her lead and kept her stride.

At age 11: competing at a summer sports event

A man ran out into the middle of the road and dumped a bucket of water on her head. Thelma sped for the finish. Almost a mile to go. Her legs were starting to cramp from the cold water and now she had to worry about her pants. The weight of the water was pulling them down. Watch out for hoses, men with buckets, inhale the fumes, but keep going, keep running.

A soaking wet Thelma Wright crossed the finish line first, one full minute ahead of the next runner, establishing a new record for the marathon of thirty-five minutes and forty-three seconds. The three Canadian women had stolen the show. Her compatriots had taken both second and fourth places.

As she boarded the plane carrying her trophy, Thelma smiled to herself. If anyone asks how it was at the Puerto Rico marathon, I'll just tell them, Six and a quarter miles, no problem.

Thelma has had plenty of experience putting problems out of her head. When she was fourteen, her parents separated. Her mother left their home in western Canada and went to England. A few months later she wrote Thelma that she would not be coming back. Her fifteen year old brother left home later that same summer. Years later he turned up in Tibet, where he is now studying to be a Buddhist monk.

The loss of half of her family didn't keep Thelma from becoming a winner on the track. She won the 880-yard event in her first official competition, one of the largest high school track meets in North America. She had found something she could pour her energy into. She would find just how far she could go—and how fast.

Her father observed her interest in running. He became

Thelma in Italy, September, 1971

involved as a director of her track club, helped with timing at meets and assisted with some of the coaching. He found that it worked better if he didn't coach her, but Thelma couldn't stop him from telling everyone he met about her accomplishments. He was so proud.

He had much to be proud of. Thelma brought home athletic and academic honors by the bushel. She was the outstanding graduate and valedictorian of her high school class and earned a scholarship to the University of British Columbia, where she graduated with the second highest grades in her class. On her way through school, she won a whole roomful of trophies and medals for her running. One bronze medal from the 1970 Commonwealth Games was awarded to her by Prince Phillip. Seven times in the last nine years five foot, ninety-eight pound Thelma was named the outstanding university track athlete in Canada.

She married Lee Wright in her junior year in college. Although she's been a wife for four years, only two have been spent with her husband because of an intensive schedule which has included training and competing all over the globe. Lee has encouraged her to reach for her full potential. As a field hockey player who competed in the 1964 Olympics, he understands the thrills and sacrifices involved in serious competition. So when Thelma mentioned quitting, he told her she would always regret it if she didn't go to the Olympic Games.

At the 1972 Games she didn't run as well as she could but still she was always surrounded by admiring youngsters. Amid the autograph books thrust at her one day was a very crumpled piece of paper. Thelma looked up to see who handed it to her. Her husband smiled and said, "Hi, I just wanted to say hello."

His understanding is very important to Thelma who is beginning to feel pressure from people who urge her to settle down, spend more time with Lee and start a family now that she is twenty-four. She disagrees with the idea that a woman should give up her own competitive drive and only be interested in what her husband does.

There have been times when Thelma longs for a "normal life." During the lonely painful workouts, or when she's fighting to get back in shape after a pulled hamstring muscle, she finds herself questioning the tremendous effort required. But deep inside she knows it's all worth it.

Her life outside track is very important. She feels there will be plenty of time later to start a family and she looks forward to it. "We are the lucky sex," she says. "We can give birth to another life, another chance to enjoy life to the fullest!"

When it comes to the events offered by the Olympics, Thelma does not feel quite so much like the "lucky" sex. She's very upset that there is no 3000 meter race for women. "It's ridiculous having a 1500 meter be the maximum race. For some of that's almost like a sprint."

She enjoys competing against men when she has the chance. In one cross country six mile road race in Vancouver she was the first female, 28th overall, in a group of 380 runners. The next woman was 171st. "Boy," she said, "did that feel good beating all those guys. Especially the ones who couldn't believe a girl would beat them."

She feels women have greater potential than they are

Thelma with her
coach, Lionel Pugh,
September, 1971,
in Italy

With friends in
London, England,
after finishing her
race, July, 1975

using. Thelma is glad she was brought up in Canada, where track and field is a combined sport; there is one team with members of both sexes rather than separate men's and women's teams. The result is that Canadian women get equal opportunities to use first rate facilities and to have topnotch coaching.

No one deserves first rate opportunities more than Thelma Wright.

TWO Joni Huntley

"Hey, Joni, I bet you can't do that."

Joni Huntley's brother lay flat on his back grinning up at the bampoo pole above him. The pole hadn't even wobbled. It was the first time he had cleared it at that height. Jerry had been trying for two weeks, but until today he hadn't been able to do it.

"I don't know, Jerry. I don't think my legs are long enough."

"You want me to put it down a notch for you?"

"No, leave it there. I'll try it." Nine-year-old Joni took a deep breath and ran toward the pole. But she was off balance when she reached it, so she ducked and ran under it.

"You're supposed to go over the bar, not under it." Jerry was eleven and liked giving advice to his younger sister.

"Really, Jerry? I didn't know that." Joni giggled. "Is that what they teach you in sixth grade?"

Joni looked at the bar and said to herself. "I can do that. Last time Jerry said I cleared it by a couple of inches."

Joni Huntley relaxing before a race
in North Carolina in 1975

She ran and jumped. The seat of her jeans touched the bar. It trembled but it didn't fall.

Jerry was impressed. "How'd you do that?" He'd been practicing every day and was usually several notches ahead of Joni.

"I learned it in fourth grade," she kidded.

They both laughed. Their school didn't have a jumping pit. Sheridan, Oregan, was such a small town that even the high school had no track. When kids tried out for the Junior Olympics, they ran in the road in front of the school. Jerry and Joni had watched them from behind wooden barriers that blocked the traffic from the street.

It was a good feeling to have jumped as high as Jerry. He always seemed to be better than she was. But at least he let her come along when he practiced. Her friends didn't think spending the afternoon running and jumping at the playground was fun.

Joni and Jerry put their homemade jump standard on their bikes and rode home to tell their parents the news.

"How did you do it, Joni?" her dad asked. "Jerry's been trying to reach that notch for a couple weeks, but I didn't think you were ready for it."

"Well," Joni said, "I cleared the bar by at least a couple inches when I made the last notch so I figured I could do it. The first time I tried I was thinking my legs were too short, but I never make it when I think that way. The second time I thought I could do it and I did."

Her Dad smiled. "I hope it's always that easy for you."

It hasn't been "that easy" for Joni Huntley.

She remembers her first track meet well. "In the 50-yard dash at the State Junior Olympics meet, I zigzagged

During Pan American competitions, 1975

Two views of Joni establishing a six-foot jumping
record for Oregon high school competitions, 1974

in and out to get ahead of the other girls. I was so disapointed when they disqualified me. I thought all you had to do to win was to run faster than everybody else. Nobody ever told me I had to stay in my lane."

Joni made up for that disappointment many times during her high school career. When she was a freshman she jumped 5'3" and placed third in the state high school meet. Every meet after that she improved a quarter of an inch. By her sophomore year she reached 5'6". That seemed fine to her until she saw a Jamaican girl clear 6 feet at the AAU Nationals.

"I couldn't believe I was watching a woman jump six feet," she said. She went home and practiced more seriously.

Her high school had no high jump facilities. For track meets they set up a temporary pit in the parking lot. But each week in her senior year her parents drove her a hundred miles round trip so she could practice in a real jumping pit.

Joni astounded them and everyone else at the Oregon High School Track Meet in her senior year where she scored all thirty-two team points for Sheridan High. She placed first in the high jump and long, second in the 100-yard dash and fourth in the 100-meter hurdles. While she was at it, she set two national records, one in the 100-yard hurdles and one in the high jump. When she cleared the bar at six feet, 18 year-old Joni Huntley became the first American woman ever to do so.

This attractive auburn-haired one-woman track team was honored for her accomplishments at the state's Annual Banquet of Champions. She was awarded both the Hayward Trophy as Oregon's outstanding amateur athlete of 1974 and the Oregon High School Athlete of the Year Award. She became the first person ever to win both honors in the same year and only the third woman to win the Hayward trophy, the highest award given in the state to either a male or female.

Suddenly lots of reporters wanted to interview Joni, but she felt uncomfortable talking about herself. "I'm just like anyone else except I happen to excel in one particular thing," she told them.

Her father said, "We're grateful Joni didn't become a spoiled brat when the publicity and honors came her way as some athletes do. We've tried to teach our children to respect others and work hard."

Joni knows all about working hard. When she started high school she changed her jumping style from the foot-first scissors to the flop in which the feet go over the bar last. At first she didn't want to make the change. She was satisfied with jumping 4'10''. But her physical education teacher took her to a college to see a film on the flop technique. With a printed sheet of instructions and a great deal of help from her teacher and her father, Joni finally mastered the head-first jump.

At Oregon State University her training includes running up and down the stadium seats and working out with weights. "I don't enjoy the weight workouts but knowing they are helping means I don't hate them so much," she says.

Sometimes she gets discouraged. There are no indoor facilities, and it's hard to work out when it's cold, especially in the rain or snow. "I really get tired of training by myself all the time. In the fall, when there aren't any meets, I feel like quitting. During practice I can't even jump 5 feet because my legs are so dead from the strength work I do. As soon as I go to my first meet, however, I know why I didn't quit."

Worse than loneliness and cold is the pain. Joni says, "Sometimes I could drop because I hurt so much. I've got a bad back and jumping hurts it. I've gone through a lot of pulled muscles, shin splints, and just plain fatigue. I hate being injured, but I haven't yet reached the limit my body can tolerate."

There have been frustrations, too. Sometimes she's been pushed and hurried during competition in order to accomodate the male jumpers. Many times the pits are set up to facilitate the men, and women are not allowed to adjust them to fit their approaches. And it bothers her when huge crowds turn out for the men's competitions and hardly anyone shows up for the women's track events. She's hoping this will change as women's track and field competitions rise in spectator popularity as golf and tennis have done.

Joni's experiences have been mostly positive. The head coach for the men at her university has taken time to help her whenever she's wanted it. The men on the college high jump team have been supportive, too. She'll continue jumping because her sport means so much to her. By attending meets all over the world, she's met different types of people and made many friends.

One of her most exciting moments took place in New Zealand where she completed her highest jump on record — 6 feet, 2¾ inches.

Joni is convinced that always striving to become better and meeting new challenges have made her a stronger person. And there's nothing to compare with that tingly

Joni and friends representing the United States
in Odessa, Russia, July, 1973

feeling she gets inside when standing on top of the awards stand.

Like many college girls, Joni, who is 5'8" tall, likes eating and talking and has lots of friends. She enjoys school and does well. In her spare time she enjoys macrame, sewing and working with plants. Someday she hopes to become a physical education teacher and administrator.

"I'm very interested," she says "in trying to help other women athletes to be able to achieve. So many young women try to rush it. It takes time and practice."

Joni is not ready to settle into a career just yet. She sees jumping as a personal challenge and still hopes to try for that world record.

THREE Robin Campbell

"Robin, I thought I asked you to go to the store for me. Now hurry, we need that bread for supper."

Robin put the brown paper bag on the kitchen counter with a grin. "Here it is, Mom."

"You mean you're back already?" Her mother looked surprised. "You just left."

"I knew you needed it for supper. Besides, I like to see how fast I can run. It's fun."

Robin Campbell has had a lot of fun. She's also been a winner. And she owes it all to her love of running.

There's a sign in her room that reads, "Winning isn't everything, but losing is nothing."

She found out when she was nine what winning could do for her. And she's been finding out ever since.

When she was in fourth grade, Robin joined her elementary school track team. At a meet held in her hometown, Washington, D.C., she met Olympian long jumper Martha Watson.

"There's a man here you should know. Come on, I'll introduce you," Martha said.

Coach Brooks Johnson seemed glad to meet Robin. "I watched you win that race. How would you like to join our club team?"

Robin wasn't sure what a club team was so she told him she'd ask her parents. He gave her a paper with his phone number written on it. Her mother and father asked what she'd like to do.

"I just want to run," she answered.

Her dad laughed. "Okay, Robin, then you should run. I'll call Mr. Johnson and tell him to sign you up."

After joining Sports International Track Club, Robin had more chances to run that she'd ever dreamed possible. She found out it wasn't all fun.

"I usually practice two times a day and that's hard work," she says. "No one likes to feel pain, but I decided that there's no way in the world I can be the best in my event if I don't suffer."

Hard work, long hours of conditioning, and the desire to be the best have paid off. She began to win races at some of the more important meets. Doors started to open for Robin, doors she is still running through.

She achieved almost instant fame when she was fourteen by winning the half mile race against the Russians in her first international competition in March, 1973, at Richmond, Virginia. She surprised everyone; no one had expected much of such a young runner.

Having gained a reputation as one of the best women's middle-distance runners in the world, Robin found new opportunities developing. At sixteen she was the youngest member of the AAU (Amateur Athletic Union) track team to tour China. As a part of a school assignment she kept a journal on the trip:

Receiving trophy after selection as outstanding female
athlete, 17th Annual Marine Corps Relays.

They gave us a twelve course Chinese meal. Man, I was full after the appetizers. Every time somebody would start to give a talk, the Chinese would all lay down their chopsticks to listen, but the Americans would keep on eating. Pretty soon we figured out about putting down our sticks, too.

When someone talked or gave a toast everybody would say "kam pei" which means "empty your glass." But I said "Not me," and I kept drinking my orange juice. That wine, or whatever it was, looked too strong. They served squid and I liked the mushrooms and the rice. But I was wishing for a McDonald's and some french fries or maybe a taco.

The Americans were photographed all the time, even when they were just warming up. The Chinese hoped to learn something that would help them get into the Olympic Games. But Robin said, "They do everything the same way at the same time in the same uniform. I don't think they should try to copy our form. If they do, they're in bad shape because everybody here has a different style."

She is the first to admit she has the "worst form." Her coach says, "Robin is not a natural runner. Her mechanics are pretty bad. She has made it by tough work, application and competitiveness." Robin adds that her talent for running is a "gift from God."

An elderly Chinese woman who had had her feet bound as a child made a lasting impression on Robin. She could only take one or two steps because her feet were too small to support her body. Robin was horrified that people would do that to something as precious as their feet.

She feels lucky to have seen so much of the world. "The best part of running track for me is the travel," she says. "My mother and dad have seven children and they can't afford to take us many places. I hate to read about people in other countries and never get to see them. Now I'm getting the chance. When I first left the United States I thought I was in a dream. I kept thinking I'd see my house around every corner."

Robin winning the women's 440-yard dash in the US vs USSR track meet in Richmond, Va., Spring, 1975

Robin watches intently from the stands, August 1970

Both Robin's parents work full time and agree that it is a strain to finance an amateur athlete. They are grateful for the contributions their friends and co-workers have been making ever since their daughter started running. And they have no regrets about their own sacrifices because they want all their children to be able to look back on their childhoods with happy memories.

Her father tries to take the other children to see Robin run. "It costs a lot," he admits. "But they're being exposed to different lifestyles. I tell Robin she is opening doors for other young black women."

Robin knows that the money doesn't come easily. "Even though my parents try to treat us equally, I know I'm getting the most financial support. Someday I want to get a job and make a lot of money so I can take them to all the places I've seen." She shares her experiences with her brothers and sisters and always remembers to bring them gifts from her travels.

The Campbells are a close family and Robin's appreciation of her life at home has grown along with her success. She thinks most teenagers can't wait to grow older so they can move into their own place, but because she's traveled so much, she doesn't feel that way. In fact, she'd like more time just to enjoy being part of the family.

Not that she doesn't like to get out of some of the work! She used to hope track meets would fall on Monday night when she was supposed to do the dishes. Then when she traveled she thought she might get out of doing them completely. But when she got home, she found she was scheduled for a whole week to make up the times she'd missed.

When her coach transferred the track club to Florida to take advantage of the warmer weather for year round practice, she wasn't sure she wanted to leave home. Her parents had mixed feelings about the move, too. She was only sixteen, but they knew Coach Johnson was doing the best thing for her career. Robin said, "I went because I figured if I didn't go, I wouldn't know what I really could do."

Coach Johnson enrolled Robin and her younger sister at Oak Hill, a private school where the Campbell sisters were the only blacks. He feels that academics are always more important than athletics.

Robin at 16, the youngest member of the U.S. Track and Field Team, with young Chinese spectators before a practice session in Shanghai, Spring, 1975

"The work load was awesome," he said. "Robin would go into a final exam with a B plus, draw a blank and come out with a C. The pressure was difficult for her to cope with. She went to China for forty-five days and still got four A's and a B in Washington. At Oak Hill School we were afraid if we let her go to Russia for seven days she wouldn't be able to keep a C."

Fortunately, Robin has been able to keep up her grades and work hard on her running, too. Her concentrated training has produced good results; she ran in a world-record relay and has been a consistent winner. Her coach is very proud of her. "She's the only runner," he says "ever to have national qualifying times in every event from the 220 yard dash to the two mile run."

Robin considers her coach the most influential person in her life. She knows he wants the best for her even when he insists she go to practice instead of a party or when he encourages her to eat nutritious food rather than the junk food she loves. "I know it's bad for my teeth," she says "and it puts on weight but I could eat candy bars and ice cream sodas all the time."

Like many other teenagers, seventeen year-old Robin likes to crochet, bike, play badminton, shop, and chat on the phone. Friends are very important to her. The worst thing about track is having to race against girls she knows and likes. If she accidentally bumps someone in a race, she always turns and says "O, excuse me".

Her high school friends admire her and have nick-named her Superstar. She's found that boys respect her ability and those who like to run usually want to race against her. "I have nothing to prove," says Robin, "so I will never compete against men except for fun."

Robin running in Van Cortland Park (New York, New York) in 1972

She feels that the Olympics are unfair to women because they don't offer as many events as for the men. For instance, there is no women's marathon.

When it comes to competition, Robin believes in giving a hundred per cent effort. Does she get nervous? Robin laughs. "I bite my fingernails and swallow my bubblegum. It seems as if I only have enough energy to run my race. Anything I do before a race makes me really tired. If I tie my shoe string or cough before I run, it seems as if I have used all my energy and have to prepare myself all over again."

But prepare herself she does. And when she gets going, watch out. Because Robin Campbell can still bring home a loaf of bread faster than anyone around.

FOUR Kathy Schmidt

"Out!" the umpire called. "You're out."

Kathy felt a glow of pride. She'd heaved the ball from deep in center field with all her strength. It had beat the runner home. Her teammate congratulated Kathy as she reached the bench. "Wow, Kathy, terrific! You've got some arm."

Her coach said, "Your throw is the reason we won this game. But even more important is that arm of yours. I want to talk to you about it on the way home."

Kathy looked down at her arm. It was the same one she'd had for thirteen years. Suddenly it seemed special.

On the bus the coach said, "Kathy, you ought to consider trying the javelin. You really have an exceptional throwing arm. With good coaching you could go a long way."

When she told her parents what her coach had said, they didn't share her enthusiasm. They thought she might be better off putting more energy into her school work.

That settled it. She'd do it anyway. She'd prove to them she could "go a long way." Her hands itched to get hold of a javelin.

49

Kathy Schmidt, February, 1976

Kathy soon learned there was more to javelin throwing than talent and hard work. The Long Beach, California, schools she attended didn't have any facilities or programs for would-be javelin throwers. Luckily she was able to join a local track team, the **Long Beach Comets.** The coach, Dave Pearson, taught Kathy the basics of throwing and gave her some much-needed encouragement. Her first track meet was an experience she would never forget. A whole new world opened up, a world she came to love.

When she was sixteen, Kathy injured her elbow by throwing off balance during competition. The doctor who treated her was very grave. "You've torn the tendon," he said. "I don't like to be the one to tell you this, but I have to. You'll never throw again."

Kathy couldn't believe her ears. Never throw again! But she had just begun to master the sport. She couldn't stop now.

In desperation she consulted another doctor. He came to the same conclusion as the first. Finally she found one who offered hope. There was some scar tissue making a connection to the bone. Maybe, if she was careful and began to train gradually after a long rest period . . .

Kathy didn't have to hear any more. When she finally began exercises the pain was incredible. But slowly the power began returning and soon she was throwing again. Two years later a very determined Kathy Schmidt threw her javelin far enough to break the American record.

Javelin throwers must cope with plenty of aches even when they are not injured. "Even a near-perfect throw hurts," says Kathy. "And if everything isn't just right, the speed and explosion of the throw can easily injure the arm. This sport has tremendously increased the amount of pain I can tolerate."

One way to keep the pain at a bearable level is to stay in top physical condition. Weight-lifting and running are as important to Kathy's training program as throwing. She alternates weight-lifting days with throwing days and runs three times a week.

Pain and injury are problems, but they are not quite so complicated as the whole question of being a woman in a traditionally masculine sport. Kathy has found that javelin throwing women are not as readily accepted as figure skaters and tennis players. Some people still have that old troublesome idea that sports make a man more of a man but a woman less of a woman.

Kathy is tall, six foot-one, and very attractive. She has long brown hair and a beautiful smile. When she's not involved with sports, she enjoys reading and writing poetry.

Boys and men react to her in different ways. Kathy says, "If they have any confidence in themselves, they appreciate what I'm doing. If they know me, it helps a great deal. If they don't know me and don't feel good about themselves, they see me as a threat."

Most of her boyfriends are track athletes. They have been very helpful and encouraging. She says, "We work out together, help coach each other, and share our victories and defeats."

Does she ever feel discriminated against in training or competing because she's female? "Yes, all the time. Right now I'm trying to help establish the track program at UCLA. The hours that women can use the track are atrocious."

But the picture is not all bleak. A woman's weight room has been built and there is more money for facilities than there has been in past years. Kathy feels confident that the future of all women's sports is tremendous, but that before women can come into their own, some things must be changed. One of the biggest barriers, she feels, is the Amateur Athletic Union. This is an old organization which was founded in 1888 to promote amateur athletics and set up standards for sports. Kathy, along with many other athletes, feels they are too tied up in politics and have lost sight of their original goals.

Despite the problems, there are plenty of plusses for Kathy in track and field competition. She likes winning, keeping physically fit, being outdoors and, most of all, making friends on the track circuit. "My career has been a growing, learning experience," she says. "Everything traumatic, painful, disappointing, wonderful, and glorious has been a part of what has made me happy for eight years. I don't regret any of it. If I had a choice I would do all of it over again."

A high point was the 1972 Olympic Games at Munich. She says, "I felt like I was in another world, on another planet. I can't describe what it's like being surrounded by 10,000 of the best physical specimens in the world."

Kathy's had plenty of pleasure from winning. She's set the American record a number of times and won silver medals in the 1973 and 1975 World University Games. In international competition she's won so many medals she's lost count. At the 1972 Olympics when she placed third, she became the first American woman in forty years to bring home a medal for the javelin throw. The achievement that still means the most to her was the first time

Kathy at the Bakersfield Nationals, June, 1974

she set the American record. When she did that—March, 1972, at Valencia—she became the first woman from the United States to throw more than two hundred feet. She won still another medal—a bronze—at the 1976 Montreal Olympics for a javelin throw of 209', 10.1". This did not come up to her American record throw of 215', 6", made on March 6, 1976, at the Long Beach relays.

Kathy has certainly lived up to her softball coaches prediction that she could "go a long way."

FIVE Jane Frederick

Jane was slow off the starting block for the 100-meter hurdle race. She was running second by about a foot. Then she shot over the last hurdle with a burst of speed that put her in front at the finish.

A friend congratulated her on the victory. "You looked good. I didn't think you were going to pull it out."

"I just wanted it," Jane explained. "I couldn't afford to fall behind. There's a long day ahead."

Jane is a pentathlete whose track "event" is really five events. After the hurdles she competed in the shot put. Next, it was the high jump. Then the long jump and, last, the 200-meter dash.

Yes, it was a long day of competition—the National Pentathlon Championships at Los Alomos in the spring of 1975—but it turned out to be a worthwhile one. She gave a nearly flawless demonstration of mental as well as physical preparedness. She led three events and was a close second in the other two. As a result she shattered her American record with 4676 points, more than 200 points over the existing record.

A smiling and happy winner, Jane waves to the crowds
after a leading jump of 20 feet, 10 inches at Eugene,
Oregon in June, 1972

Jane, immediately after hurling the shot.

Jane first became interested in track and field when she was eleven. She liked it all—the running, the throwing, and the jumping. In fact, one of her first problems was which one she should concentrate on.

When she told her parents she had joined the track club at school they were pleased, especially her dad, who was a university track official.

"Which event do you think I should choose?" Jane asked him.

"There's no need to choose only one, especially at your age. Maybe you'll be a pentathlete."

Jane took her father's advice and went on to become our National Woman's Champion in the pentathlon. She also took her mother's advice, which was that there is more to life than running, jumping, and throwing. Her mom encouraged her to study and develop her artistic and literary talents.

All through her high school years Jane worked hard on her studies and developed her track skills. No time for fun? Jane's idea of a good time is working toward her goals. She enjoys the process of training and studying as much as the achievements. And there have been many payoffs.

Jane graduated with honors from the University of Colorado where she majored in Italian and minored in German. She is one of the few American athletes who can carry on a fluent conversation in another language at international meets.

She remembers one afternoon she spent in the stands at the Munich Olympics chatting with some East German athletes. They began making some very elaborate paper airplanes.

"I've never seen such beautiful paper planes," she said in German.

They smiled and looked very proud; they made some even more complicated models.

"In the United States we make them like this," she said, quickly folding the wings back. "Your planes are a tribute to the famous German industrial precision."

The only trouble with those complex and intricately made airplanes was, as Jane remembered, that none of them flew.

Jane in the People's Republic of China, June, 1975

Jane holds award she received in 1975 at the World University Track and Field Games in Rome. She took the pentathlon with 4,442 points, giving the United States one of two gold medals.

Jane likes to converse with athletes from other countries. "Everyone thinks the Russians are cold and unfriendly, but they aren't if you talk with them," she says. Some of Jane's most rewarding moments have been those times she's been able to communicate in another language even if it's only to complain about the conditions of the track. She is flattered when athletes of other countries learn to rely on her linguistic skills and come to her for advice.

She became so proficient in Italian that she was able to live in Italy for a year supporting herself as an interpreter and translator while she trained under the Italian national pentathlon coach. She hopes someday to get her PhD in Italian and to have a career in the foreign service.

Her artistic talents have led her into jewelry making. Besides track and language study, it's her most enjoyable activity. "It's totally relaxing," she says. "I can be absorbed in it for hours." Jane is also an amateur photographer who can do her own darkroom work. In her spare time she is learning to play the banjo.

All her activities are scheduled around her training which takes about three hours a day. In the fall she starts general conditioning exercises. January and February are devoted to strength and running plus technique drilling. Spring means more drills and sometimes going through the whole event. During May and June she sharpens her performance in preparation for the July and August competitions.

She feels that physical pain is not the problem that mental pain is. "I never work so hard that I mentally harm myself," she says. "A contented mind can take a great deal of physical abuse. A mind that is strained can not."

Whenever workouts cause too much physical pain, she eases off. If she begins to feel conflicts between her training and activities she would enjoy more, she sits down and talks with herself. "If I can't mentally or emotionally justify the denials, then I rearrange my schedule. Usually I keep at it because I know I have more potential to develop."

She credits at least part of her success to weight lifting. "Usually," she says, "you get the benefits of hard work the year after. I feel much more stable now. It's starting to come together."

At twenty-five Jane is an attractive five-foot eleven-inch blonde. She's had to ignore a lot of social pressure from people who feel the pentathlon is not as valid an activity for a woman as it is for a man. Many have questioned the great amounts of time and energy she'd devoted to something so "physical."

She's been interested in the reaction of boys and men. Most are impressed because they find it hard to believe a girl can meet the rigorous demands of the events and excel at all of them. Some boys have been intimidated by her success but Jane says, "I just leave them to their hangups." As for her boyfriends, she says, "They have loved me for all that I do and care about. Otherwise we wouldn't get along."

Jane's very comfortable with herself and her sport. She feels women's achievements are as remarkable and interesting to women as men's are to men. She sees no need to compar them. But she does regret the huge barrier erected by our culture which prevents young girls

Representing the Los Angeles Track Club at Olympic trials at Eugene, Oregon, 1976.

from being interested in track and field, particularly in such a grueling activity as the pentathlon. "Often," she says, "athletic women are channeled into a more 'appropriate' sport. I get tired of people saying that what I do isn't feminine."

Jane gets results because she's willing to work hard. Deciding who she is and what she is willing to do to get what she wants has always been important to her. At the 1972 Olympic Games she said, "I saw what I had to do to get where I wanted to go and I decided to do it."

Jane considers herself a pentathlete first and foremost because "my mentality, my personality don't go with one event." She likes to know that "it's just me out there, no team, no contact, just me and my performance compared to others and their performances under the same conditions."

She is the epitome of the versatile athlete who knows who she is and what she wants. That kind of woman is hard to stop.

SIX Patty van Wolvelaere

Patty glanced at the clock on the wall—2:35. Why did it move so slowly? She couldn't wait to get to practice. Today she would run faster than ever before. She felt strong. She felt . . .

"Patty." Her English teacher's voice brought her back to reality. "My guess is your mind is more on the clock than it is on your work."

Patty put her eyes on the text but her mind flew to the track. Yesterday she'd broken her record. The time was not official because it hadn't been a meet, but now she knew what she could do.

She stole another glance. Hurry, clock, she thought.

The clock hurried and years of training and competing followed, years of travel and winning, ribbons, medals, trophies—hours and hours of the pure joy of running.

Bad times? The Munich Olympics had been a very bad time. She had been running well in the preliminary heat, but she leaned for the finish line too soon and lost her balance. She took second place, but it was embarrassing to skid down the track on her chest. Patty Van Wolvelaere is a champion hurdler, and a champion always picks herself up when she falls. But all the will in the world couldn't heal her strained ligaments in time for the semi-finals. She ran, but came in fifth. Only the first four went on to the final Olympic competition.

Four years of work. Four years of training and conditioning. Four years of dreaming of the Olympics. And she had torpedoed it all in one day by falling on her face.

Patty is not a quitter. It would take more than a few falls to stop her. "Next time," she promised herself. "Next time I'll do it. I know I can."

It meant hard work, but she was not afraid of work. "Training is like building a house," she says. "You must have a good foundation, or what you put up is not going to stand. I like to be strong. My strength is one of the biggest assets in my hurdling."

She runs three or four days a week, sometimes as much as three miles at a time. She spends many hours working with weights and doing exercises for flexibility. Sprinting is also important. "The hurdle race," she says, "is just a sprint with barriers to overcome. A hurdler must be a sprinter." In spite of the pounding and intense work involved in hurdling, she practices several times a week. "You can't half-stride the hurdles," she explains. "You must go all out when working on them."

That's how Patty does things—all out. That's why she's a winner. Top physical condition in itself, she realizes, is not enough. "My body is my temple," she says, "but I also have a strong faith in myself and the goodness that runs this world. I think there's something to be said for the universal life energy that everyone possesses. Each of us is a total unit of physical and mental power. There

Patty practicing at San Clemente High School,
August, 1971

Patty poses for picture in January, 1974

Patty and friends during Indoor Dual Meet, USA vs. USSR, Richmond, Va., March, 1972. L to R: Kathy Hammond, Lacey O'Neil, Wendy Koeing, Iris Davis, Patty Johnson, Martha Watson, Jarvis Scott

has to be some connection between the physical and spiritual world. My religion is the totality of all the positive forces that I am able to generate within my body and within my soul."

So when Patty steps up to the starting line, an important part of the race has already begun in her mind. "I'm usually very confident, even if in reality my chances are slim. I believe I can win. I put no ceilings on my expectations."

Dedicated training and positive thinking have taken Patty a long way since the restless days in high school when she couldn't wait for track practice. She's been on every continent, has even stood on the Great Wall of China. And she holds dozens of national titles and records.

At twenty-six she's considered the 'old veteran' because of her many years of participating in international athletics. Competitors often look to her for leadership. At times she feel the pressure of having to live up to her 'superstar' image, but her position also gives her a unique opportunity to re-educate people on what it is to be a female athlete.

She likes to speak to groups of young women athletes because it gives her a chance to reassure them of their respectability and the value of a strong, positive, physical self. She doesn't need a formal speaking engagement to get started.

"I'm teaching this everywhere I go," she says, "on planes, on trains, and in restaurants. Many people think that being an athlete puts our femininity in jeopardy. That's why the female athlete is still the victim of the double standard. Males run free on trips and females

Patty wins 60-yard hurdles against Russians in
March, 1973.

have a curfew. Our chaperones are afraid we'll hurt our feminine image."

Patty understands the kinds of pressure young girls are under. Five years ago she was working out in the rain wearing a hooded rain parka. A young boy sneered at her and yelled, "What are you anyway, a boy or a girl?"

Patty says, "Now I can understand and see it as a chance to educate him, but at the time I was outraged and offended by his attitude."

She says that some people see being strong, aggressive, and in control of one's life as masculine. In the past women tried to adjust themselves to this idea. But the idea should be changed, not the women. She encourages women to be proud of their strengths.

There is another problem that makes female athletes valued less than their male counterparts. "We don't get as much exposure as men do, so it's hard to change the public's mind about women athletes. Also, we don't get the chance for good competition often enough to maintain high levels of performance.

"Even though I'm the indoor world record holder in the sixty-yard indoor hurdles, I often have trouble getting a hurdle race included in the big meets here in Los Angeles. Since this is my home, it wouldn't cost the promoters any expense money to get me. Yet they'll often fly a lesser caliber male athlete across the country if his name is known because that will increase gate receipts. Women don't get enough publicity to make their names known well enough to draw crowds. Since they don't produce revenue, they aren't treated with the respect men are. We end up getting inferior facilities, inferior officials, and the worst hours to work out on the track. It's a vicious circle."

In spite of these problems, Patty likes to point out that there are some great opportunities beginning to develop for women in sports—scholarships, attitudes that are gradually changing, and expanding job opportunities that include broadcasting, coaching, and sports writing.

With new worlds opening up to women all the time, she is sad to see so many high school girls out of shape and out of touch with their bodies. They take meticulous care of their face, hair, and nails, yet they seem to ignore the rest. She urges them to experience the joy that comes from exercise.

Patty is eager to have others share the happiness and satisfaction she's found in living, both on and off the track.

ABOUT THE AUTHOR

A professional writer and teacher of writing, Diana Gleasner is a former physical education teacher whose life-long interest in sports has resulted in two books in the Women in Sports Series —**Swimming** and **Track and Field.** Her husband is a photographer and together they form a photo-journalism team whose stories and pictures have appeared in home, sports, and travel magazines. The Gleasners, with their two children, are currently living in Hawaii.